TO FLY

THE STORY OF THE WRIGHT BROTHERS

Wilbur Wright.   Orville Wright

by Wendie Old

ILLUSTRATED BY ROBERT ANDREW PARKER

· · ·

CLARION BOOKS *New York*

For my granddaughter, Ariana—in hopes that she will love to fly as much as I do.
—*W. O.*

For my mother, Harriet Cowdin Parker, born in May 1903.
—*R. A. P.*

Clarion Books
a Houghton Mifflin Company imprint
215 Park Avenue South, New York, NY 10003
Text copyright © 2002 by Wendie Old
Illustrations copyright © 2002 by Robert Andrew Parker

The illustrations were executed in watercolor.
The text was set in 18-point Goudy.
Designed by Janet Pedersen.

www.houghtonmifflinbooks.com

"Crazy Boys" by Beverly McLoughland first appeared in *Hand in Hand: An American History Through Poetry,*
edited by Lee Bennett Hopkins (New York: Simon & Schuster, 1994). Used by permission of the author.

Printed in Singapore

Library of Congress Cataloging-in-Publication Data

Old, Wendie C.
To fly : the story of the Wright brothers / by Wendie Old ; illustrated by Robert Andrew Parker.
p. cm.
Includes bibliographical references and index.
Summary: Traces the work that the two Wright brothers did together to develop the first machine-powered aircraft.
ISBN 0-618-13347-X
1. Wright, Orville, 1871-1948—Juvenile literature. 2. Wright, Wilbur, 1867-1912—Juvenile literature. 3. Aeronautics—United States—
Biography—Juvenile literature. 4. Inventors—United States—Biography—Juvenile literature. 5. Aeronautics—United States—History—Juvenile
literature. [1. Wright, Orville, 1871-1948. 2. Wright, Wilbur, 1867-1912. 3. Aeronautics—Biography.] I. Parker, Robert Andrew, ill. II. Title.

TL540.W7 O42 2002
629.13'0092'2—dc21
[B] 2001047219

TWP 10 9 8 7 6 5 4 3 2 1

CRAZY BOYS

Watching buzzards,
Flying kites,
Lazy, crazy boys
The Wrights. They

Tried to fly
Just like a bird
Foolish dreamers
Strange. Absurd. We

Scoffed and scorned
Their dreams of flight
But we were wrong
And they were Wright.

—Beverly McLoughland

orville   wilbur

Contents

— 1 —

DREAMS OF FLYING

$\mathcal{P}$eople had always known it wasn't possible for humans to fly like birds. But that didn't stop them from dreaming about it.

Orville Wright was one of those dreamers. Many a night he lay in his bed in Dayton, Ohio, imagining what it would be like to swoop through the sky. Sometimes in school, when he was supposed to be doing math or working on penmanship, he would be thinking about flying.

In 1878, his father brought home a toy called a Pénaud helicopter. It was made of cork, bamboo, and thin paper. When its long rubber band was wound up and then let go, the helicopter jumped out of its holder and flew almost fifty feet.

Could a person fly that way? Orville and his older brother, Wilbur, tried making more helicopters. They tried making them larger.

Miss Ida Palmer, Orville's second grade teacher, caught him fiddling with pieces of wood at his desk instead of doing classwork. Orville explained that he was making a flying machine. If it worked, he planned to build a much larger one and fly with his eleven-year-old brother.

But the boys' larger machine wouldn't fly. They had not yet learned that a machine twice as big required eight times the amount of energy to move it. For a man-sized machine, they certainly needed something stronger than a rubber band.

So they put the idea of a flying machine away. For a time.

— 2 —

KITES

Wilbur and Orville Wright had two older brothers, Reuchlin and Lorin. Their sister, Katharine, was the baby of the family.

Their father and mother, Bishop Milton Wright and Susan Wright, encouraged their five children do their own thinking. They wanted them to explore many ideas and come to their own conclusions. They even let their children take time off from school if they felt the children would learn something from the experience.

On the other hand, if the children wanted money to spend on hobbies or experiments, they had to earn it themselves. Some of their projects, like the circus the brothers put on, were successful. Others, such as the attempt to make chewing gum out of hunks of tar, were not.

One of Orville's best money-making ideas was to build kites to sell to his friends.

At first, Orville had very little money to buy supplies, so he cut the wooden ribs for the kites very, very thin. This way he could get more ribs from each piece of wood. These thin ribs bent in the wind, creating a kite with a curved surface. Orville's kites flew better than flat kites with thicker, stronger ribs.

This flying experiment was a success. Orville built the best kites in Dayton, Ohio. And he also made an important discovery that he would use later—curved wings fly better than flat ones.

— 3 —

WORKING TOGETHER

*I*n time, Orville and Wilbur's older brothers moved out into the working world and got married. But Orville and Wilbur continued to live at home. Neither of them ever married.

Wilbur finished all but the last few weeks of high school. He never graduated. He spent the next three years taking care of their sick mother. Susan Wright died of tuberculosis on July 4, 1889. After she died, their sister, Katharine, kept house for the boys and their father.

During high school, Orville had started a printing business. When their mother died, Wilbur joined him. Their newspaper advertisements read:

WRIGHT BROS.: JOB PRINTERS AT 7 HAWTHORN STREET.

This was the first time the words "Wright Brothers" appeared in print.

During his last year in high school, Orville only took one course—Latin. The rest of the time he worked in the print shop. The two brothers printed posters, business cards, and several newspapers. Orville never graduated from high school, either. Katharine, however, graduated from both high school and college. She became a teacher.

Soon a new interest took the boys' time away from the print shop—bicycles.

— 4 —

BICYCLES

The two brothers became involved in the latest fad of the 1890s—bicycles. Wilbur loved taking long rides in the country. Orville preferred racing his bike, though he seldom won. Each enjoyed the rush of wind in his face as he pedaled along. It was as close to flying as a person could get.

They both enjoyed fixing bicycles, too—so much so that they opened a bicycle shop in 1893 and moved the printing business upstairs. Here at the Wright Cycle Company they sold and repaired bicycles.

Gradually, the income from bicycles became greater than that from printing. They closed the print shop and concentrated on bicycles. They also opened a joint bank account. From then on they shared all the money they earned. Each brother took out whatever money he needed, when he needed it.

Orville and Wilbur worked together, constantly talking over ideas. Nearly everything they did came from these discussions. When one brother had an idea, the other brother would take it, play with it, enlarge and improve it, and bounce it back to the first brother. As a result, they had the advantage of two sharp minds attacking a problem.

These conversations often became shouting matches. The brothers enjoyed arguing. In fact, Wilbur once said, "I love to scrap with Orv; he's such a good scrapper."

Each brother defended his side of the argument, louder and louder. Sometimes at the end of the discussion they would discover that they had swapped sides and were now arguing on the other side of the issue. They found that by looking at all sides of a problem, everything impossible was eliminated until all that was left was the right answer.

Otto Lilienthal

— 5 —
KITES BECOME GLIDERS

In 1896, Orville almost died from typhoid. The well near their bicycle shop had become polluted, and Orville became sick from drinking the water. Wilbur immediately moved the shop to another location.

While Orville lay in bed recovering, his brother read to him. Mostly, Wilbur read about the German glider expert Otto Lilienthal, who had recently crashed and died.

Gliders! Now, that was one way to fly. As Orville grew stronger, the brothers searched libraries for more information about flight. Finally, in early 1899, the Smithsonian Institution sent them information about American flight experts.

Wilbur wrote letters to many of them. The most successful seemed to be Octave Chanute and Samuel Pierpont Langley.

Langley, head of the Smithsonian Institution in Washington, D.C., used a steam-driven motor on his fourteen-foot-long unmanned model airplanes. He called them Aerodromes. Aerodrome #5 actually flew more than a half a mile before it ran out of steam and crashed.

Chanute was to become the Wright brothers' greatest supporter. He was experimenting near Chicago with gliders that had two or more wings. One of his gliders had twelve wings. A person hanging on to a glider attempts to guide it by swinging his legs back and forth. The glider is held in the air by wind. Gradually, it falls to the ground.

Neither Langley nor Chanute could completely control the flight of his flying machine.

— 6 —

CONTROL

*F*rom their reading and discussions, Wilbur and Orville thought they had identified the problem of flight: control. How could a person *control* his flight once he was in the air? Gliders flew in a straight line. They could not be steered. But birds swooped and turned. People should be able to do that, too.

Their experience with bicycles helped. In the air and on a bicycle, the pilot/rider can turn left or right. This is called *yaw*. In the air and on a bicycle, the pilot/rider can turn over onto his side if he is not careful. This is called *roll*. But only in the air does the pilot need to control climbing up and diving down. This is called *pitch*.

The pilot of a flying machine would have to control all three movements at once. But how?

The brothers watched birds fly. Birds circle in the air by curving one wing up while the tip of the other curves down. How could a person make a flying machine do this? Orville and Wilbur chewed on this idea.

One day Wilbur sold a bicycle inner tube to a customer. The inner tube came in a long rectangular box. While he was talking to the customer, Wilbur began twisting the box. One hand twisted down while the other hand twisted up. All at once he realized what he was doing. The twisted box looked like a pair of bird's wings circling in the air.

He ran to show Orville. If they could make the wings of a two-winged glider flex like this, they could control its flight!

Orville and Wilbur built a double-winged kite to test the idea. It measured five feet from wingtip to wingtip.

In August 1899, Wilbur took the kite to a nearby lot. Wires stretched from his hands to each of the wings. These controlled the warping, or twisting, of the wings. The kite rolled to the right and to the left in the air. The neighborhood boys cheered and yelled, falling to the ground to avoid being hit when the kite dove too low. It worked! Flight could be controlled.

A larger kite should be able to carry a man. All the Wright brothers had to do was build it.

VACATIONS AT THE OUTER BANKS

Wilbur wrote to the U.S. Weather Bureau asking where winds blew strong and steady. The spot closest to Dayton was on the Outer Banks of North Carolina. For the next three years the brothers built gliders of various shapes and tested them on the Atlantic seashore near the village of Kitty Hawk.

Often children who lived nearby came to watch the strange men fly their glider. The Wright brothers did not dress in the work clothes of the islanders. They always wore business suits. And they never flew on Sundays.

Wilbur operated the wires controlling the glider. Orville took photographs or helped get the glider in the air. The postmaster of Kitty Hawk, Bill Tate, and his brother Dan helped the Wright brothers with their glider experiments.

They would throw the glider off the sand dunes. Usually, it crashed.

The Wrights would make notes and change the position of a wing or the tail. Eventually, they moved the tail to the front of the glider and called it the elevator.

Gradually, they added weight to the glider until they saw it could carry a man and still fly. But on the day in 1900 that the brothers decided to let a person fly in the glider, the winds were too weak to lift a man's weight. Dan's ten-year-old son, Tom Tate, got to ride instead. Wilbur controlled the flight from the ground with the kite wires.

In the middle of October, on their last day there, Wilbur finally took a ride on the glider. He flew down one of the three tall sand dunes called Kill Devil Hills. The elevator worked perfectly, giving him full control of the flight.

But then it was time to go home. The brothers left the 1900 glider to rot in the sand. Bill Tate's wife cut off the sateen wing coverings and made dresses for their girls.

The next year the Wrights came back with a newer and (they hoped) better flying machine.

— 8 —

THE LARGE GLIDER

*I*n the summer of 1901, the Wrights arrived on the Outer Banks with a completely new glider. It was the largest anyone had ever tried to fly. But summer was not a good time to be at the seashore. Orville's letters to Katharine were full of complaints about wild pigs and mice, and being eaten alive by mosquitoes and sand fleas.

However, their nieces and nephews loved getting mail from the vacationing uncles. Once a package arrived with a dried horseshoe crab, bottles of salty seawater, and fine seashore sand.

Unfortunately, the 1901 glider could hardly fly at all. Wilbur kept crashing it into the ground. Sand got into his mouth and eyes and hair.

When they returned to Dayton, Wilbur was depressed. He told Orville that he didn't think people would be able to fly for a thousand years. Their friend Octave Chanute wrote letters of encouragement. Of all the flight experimenters he knew—and he knew them all—Chanute believed the Wright brothers were the closest to solving the problems of flight.

— 9 —

NEW CALCULATIONS

*T*he brothers began to suspect that the air pressure tables, which every flyer used to calculate how much curve a wing needed, must be wrong. They decided they would create new tables of air pressure.

To do this, they had to experiment with many types of wing shapes, or vanes. They carefully measured and recorded the results. This was the first time anyone had tried to measure air flow and air pressure on wing shapes.

Their first attempts did not work. They made tiny metal wings of various shapes and set them up in the yard to see how the wind affected them. But the Dayton breezes were too gentle to show any differences between the shapes.

Next, they tried mounting the vanes on an old bicycle wheel rim. They attached the rim to the handlebar of a bicycle with wire. Then Orville raced the bicycle up and down the street. But it was too difficult to measure the effect the wind had on the vanes while also balancing the bicycle.

Finally, the brothers made a wind tunnel.

They put a fan inside an old washtub that had the bottom cut out of it. The air from the fan rushed through a six-foot-long rectangular box. Through a glass window on top, they could see how the wind flowed around different wing shapes. They tested over two hundred shapes and made careful notes. When they were finished, they had created new, much more accurate tables of air pressure.

The brothers discovered that some things were actually the opposite of what most people believed. For example, most people thought that a wing needed a

The Wind Tunnel

sharp front edge, to allow it to cut through the air. However, the Wright brothers discovered in their wind tunnel that a blunt, rounded front edge, with the sharper edge to the *rear* of the wing, worked better and created more lift.

Orville was thrilled. Perhaps other experimenters had failed not because success wasn't possible, but because they had been using the wrong information.

— 10 —
A GLIDER THAT FLIES UNDER CONTROL

*T*he Wright brothers built a glider using the new tables of air pressure. This time they built the peak of the wing's arc closer to the front. By September 1902, they were back at the Outer Banks. This year the brothers needed only one local helper—Dan Tate.

That fall, Wilbur finally taught Orville to fly. Orville crashed and ate sand just like Wilbur. But by the end of October both brothers had control of the three parts of flying—roll, pitch, and yaw.

Chanute and Augustus Herring visited them on the Outer Banks, bringing their own experimental gliders to try out. Their gliders did not fly well at all.

With just a few changes, the Wright brothers' glider flew very well indeed. They improved the wings, making them warp only at the ends. Now the middle part of the wing was not able to move. This created a secure place for the pilot plus an engine.

Now they were ready to build a self-propelled flying machine.

—— 11 ——

THE FLYER

$\mathcal{D}$uring the winter of 1902–03, Orville and Wilbur built a motor and propellers for their aircraft. They were so confident that it would fly that they called it the Flyer.

Other people thought that propellers should have flat blades with sharp angles and a sharp front edge to cut through the air. By experimenting in the wind tunnel, the brothers discovered that a propeller is actually like a rotating wing. Therefore, it has to be curved like a scoop and have rounded front edges. This is how propellers are made even today.

They mounted the propellers, one on each side, behind the wings to push the Flyer along. Since they were bicycle men, they used bicycle chain to connect each propeller to the motor.

None of the early automobile companies had an engine available that was as strong and as lightweight as the brothers needed. Wilbur and Orville had to design and build one themselves, which they did with the help of their bicycle mechanic, Charlie Taylor. It was made from cast aluminum, a lightweight metal.

Now all they had to do was see if it would fly.

Tightening The Chain

—12—

THE OUTER BANKS: 1903

*I*n the fall of 1903, Orville and Wilbur shipped the pieces of their new Flyer to Kill Devil Hills on the Outer Banks to test it.

Instead of living in a tent, they built two wooden hangars near the sand dunes. One was for the old 1902 glider, which they used for flight practice. In the other one they assembled the Flyer. Their beds hung overhead. The kitchen area was at the back of one hanger.

This time they covered both the top *and* bottom of each wing with cloth. This created a smooth surface that reduced wind resistance and drag. The engine was mounted on the lower wing, to the right of the pilot.

The pilot controlled the wing warping and the tail rudder with his hips, which were wedged into a wooden cradle. When he wiggled his hips, wires from the cradle moved the wings and tail.

The front elevator wings were operated by a hand control.

The engine was either on or off. There was no way to make it go faster or slower. Once the pilot turned the engine off, the aircraft became a glider, and the brothers knew they could control it as a glider.

Like all their gliders, the Flyer had no wheels. Instead, there were two skids underneath it. These skids were supposed to act like the runners of a sled, sliding along the sand during landing.

The fall of 1903 was cold and stormy. The bad weather delayed the first flight. Also, things on the Flyer kept breaking or coming loose.

While Orville took a broken propeller shaft home to Dayton to be fixed, another inventor was also attempting a manned flight.

Near Washington, D.C., Samuel P. Langley from the Smithsonian twice sent his Great Aerodrome off a houseboat in the Potomac River. The wings and propellers of his Aerodrome had sharp front edges to cut through the air. They were curved according to the old air pressure tables.

His second and last attempt was on December 8, 1903. Again, just as it did the first time, the Great Aerodrome slid off the houseboat directly into the river. It could not fly. The pilot, Charles Manly, had to be rescued from the icy water.

Langley had failed, despite receiving huge amounts of government money. Could the Wright brothers succeed using only bicycle parts and a homemade engine?

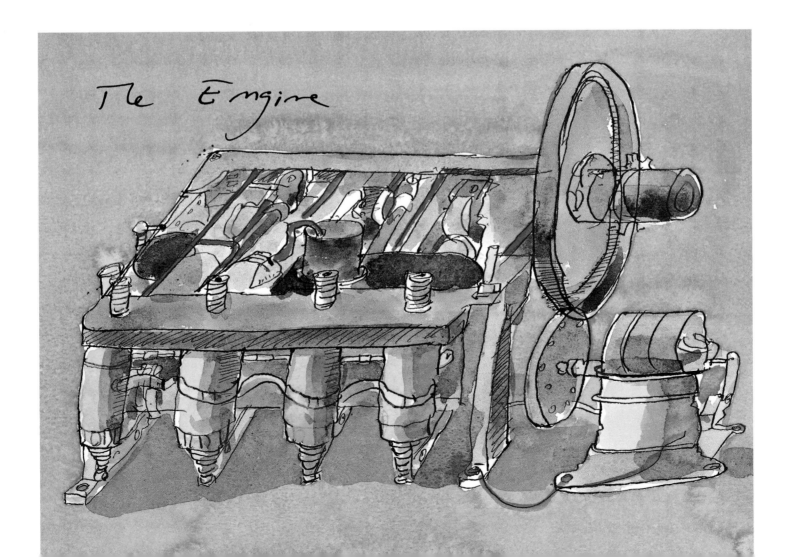
The Engine

— 13 —

THE FIRST ATTEMPT

On Monday, December 14, Orville and Wilbur Wright called the nearby Kill Devil Hills Lifesaver Corps for help. These surfmen helped to drag the Flyer partway up Big Kill Devil Hill, the largest sand dune. Because the wind was blowing at only five miles per hour, it was not strong enough to lift a glider, let alone a heavy flying machine. Gravity would help get the Flyer into the air.

The Flyer was placed at the top of a sixty-foot-long wooden rail that had been pegged into the sand. This rail would guide the Flyer until it lifted up off the ground.

Children were always attracted to both Wright brothers. The men did fascinating things, and they enjoyed having young people around. On this day, nine-year-old John Beacham, son of one of the surfmen, and his friend Caldwell played around the area with a dog while the men set up.

No one knew who would be the first pilot to fly.

Wilbur won the coin toss.

Once he was on the Flyer, Wilbur discovered that the wind was coming from the side and the track was not straight. He gave the signal to go, anyway. As soon as the awful noise of the motor started, the boys and their dog ran away.

Orville and some of the surfmen had to help the Flyer stay on the track as it sped down the hill. As soon as the Flyer lifted from the track, Wilbur turned the elevator wings up to make it go higher.

This was the wrong move. It slowed the Flyer too much. After rising only fifteen feet into the air, the Flyer stalled and slid toward the ground. The left wingtip caught in the sand. The front rudder dug deep into the sand. A few sticks in the rudder broke, plus several supports and braces.

Wilbur lay there, stunned. Finally, he managed to switch the engine off. This had not been a successful flight.

—14—
THE FIRST HEAVIER-THAN-AIR MANNED FLIGHT

*I*t took two days to repair the Flyer. The brothers were ready to go again on December 16. The men set up the rail to take off on level ground, but the wind died.

December 17 dawned freezing cold, but clear. The puddles around camp from the most recent storm had frozen. A brisk wind was blowing—between twenty and twenty-five miles per hour. This was almost too strong to be safe. But Orville and Wilbur wanted to be home for Christmas, and so they decided to try to fly anyway. This time, Orville was the pilot.

The brothers put up a red flag to summon the surfmen. Willie Dough, Adam Etheridge, and John Daniels responded. Two unexpected helpers also arrived— W. C. Brinkley, a lumber merchant from Manteo, and a boy named Johnny Moore from the nearby village of Nags Head.

The track was laid out on the flat sand. Each brother cranked a propeller. While the motor putt-putted away, the brothers stood talking a little way down the beach.

John Daniels later remembered, "After a while they shook hands, and we couldn't help notice how they held on to each other's hand, sort o' like they hated to let go; like two folks parting who weren't sure they'd ever see each other again."

At 10:35 A.M. Orville gave the signal. The Flyer began to move. Daniels

snapped a picture as the Flyer rose into the air, with Wilbur running alongside it. It's probably one of the most famous photographs ever taken.

Wilbur had asked the surfmen to cheer when the airplane took off, but Orville did not hear them. The Flyer jerked up and down, up and down. The elevator was over-responding to Orville's corrections. One hundred and twenty feet away a skid caught in the sand. It cracked. The Flyer dragged to a halt.

The first controlled heavier-than-air manned flight had lasted twelve seconds. The Flyer had taken off from level ground, moved through the air under its own power, and landed on a place that was level with its takeoff point. They had done it!

Everyone huddled by the kitchen stove in the hangar to keep warm while the cracked skid was repaired. At 11:20 A.M. it was Wilbur's turn to fly. He flew 175 feet in fifteen seconds. Then Orville flew 200 feet in the same amount of time.

Exactly at noon, the fourth flight took off. Wilbur bobbed up and down for 300 feet. Then he managed to smooth out his flight path, flying for 500 more feet before the Flyer began bobbing again and swooped to the ground. In fifty-nine seconds Wilbur had flown a total of 852 feet.

The men were excited. Despite the fact that part of the elevator frame had broken during the last landing, they talked about flying the four miles north to the village of Kitty Hawk.

John Daniels

Unfortunately, at that moment a gust of wind picked up the Flyer. Orville and John Daniels jumped to catch it. Only Daniels managed to get a firm hold.

He told people later, "I found myself caught in them wires and the machine blowing across the beach heading for the ocean, landing first on one end and then on the other, rolling over and over, and me getting more tangled up in it all the time. I tell you, I was plumb scared. When the thing did stop for half a second I nearly broke up every wire and upright getting out of it."

That afternoon Orville and Wilbur walked to the telegraph office in Kitty Hawk. They sent a telegram to their father that said:

SUCCESS FOUR FLIGHTS THURSDAY MORNING ALL AGAINST TWENTY ONE MILE WIND STARTED FROM LEVEL WITH ENGINE POWER ALONE AVERAGE SPEED THROUGH AIR THIRTY ONE MILES, LONGEST 57 SECONDS INFORM PRESS HOME [FOR] CHRISTMAS.

(By the time the telegram reached Dayton, the correct time of fifty-nine seconds had been accidentally changed to fifty-seven seconds.)

The Age of Aviation had begun.

─15─
HOME FOR CHRISTMAS

*T*he brothers packed up their equipment to return to Dayton. They took home every scrap of the wrecked 1903 Flyer and stored the crates in the back of their bicycle shop. (Years later, the Flyer was reconstructed and put on display. Today it can be seen at the Smithsonian Institution in Washington, D.C.)

They arrived home late on December 23, just in time for Christmas. Orville was so hungry for fresh milk that he immediately drank seven glasses of it.

Although the Wright family tried to notify the press of Orville and Wilbur's success, many papers refused to print the press release. Fifty-nine seconds in the air was not big enough news. Besides, people still believed that it was impossible for humans to fly. They figured that any newspaper article that claimed someone had flown must be a lie. Most were.

Four and a half years later, in 1908, Wilbur demonstrated the world's first practical working airplane in France. It could swoop. It could turn. It could fly in a figure eight. No other flying machine had this kind of control. At the same time, Orville demonstrated a Wright airplane near Washington, D.C., for the U. S. Army. These flights proved to the world that the Wright method of flying gave the pilot complete control of every motion in the air.

A newspaper in France, a year earlier, had questioned whether the brothers were "flyers or liars." Now the answer was clear.

Epilogue: It Takes Two

Scientists of the time had not been able to figure out how to make a flying machine work. People like Samuel Langley, who received more than $55,000 from the government, could not solve the problems of flight.

It took two bicycle repairmen from Dayton, Ohio, to solve them. When they made their first flight, Orville Wright was thirty-two years old; Wilbur was thirty-six.

Wilbur was an avid reader with an amazing memory. He was charming and liked talking to people. It was his idea to find out how to control flight in the air and create a practical airplane. However, he got depressed easily. Several times he was ready to give up.

Orville was shy with strangers and much more comfortable with friends and family. But it was his optimistic attitude, his way of always looking on the bright side, that kept the two of them working on the Flyer despite the setbacks.

Each brother relied on the other's strong points to counteract his own weak points.

Orville was the inventive one. He was full of ideas. To the end of his life he was always taking things apart to try to improve them.

Wilbur was the thinker. Orville would have an idea, and Wilbur would figure out how to make it work. Then Orville would improve on it. They would bounce their thoughts off each other, making the design better and better.

In this way, two young men who never graduated from high school solved mysteries that had baffled people for centuries.

When Orville Wright looked back to the years leading up to the first flight of 1903, he remembered how happy they were. Each day there was something new and exciting to discover.

Long ago, a young boy lay in bed thinking how exciting it would be to fly. On December 17, 1903, he and his brother actually did it.

A Flight Timeline

November 21, 1783 The Montgolfier brothers make world's first manned hot-air balloon flight over Paris, France.

April 16, 1867 Wilbur Wright is born in Millville, Indiana.

August 19, 1871 Orville Wright is born in Dayton, Ohio.

1877 Otto Lilienthal develops the first glider to use arched wings like a bird, much like the hang gliders we use today. He steers it by flinging his legs back and forth.

1878 Orville and Wilbur's father gives them a toy Pénaud helicopter, which sparks their interest in flying.

1885 The gasoline-powered internal-combustion engine is invented by Gottlieb Daimler in Germany. This engine is lighter and more powerful than a steam engine.

1889 Orville Wright begins publishing a weekly newspaper called the *West Side News.*

1889 The safety bicycle is introduced into the United States and becomes popular.

1893 The Wright brothers open a bicycle shop.

1894 In England, Hiram Maxim builds a huge airplane, powered by two steam engines, which glides along a wooden track. It hops off the track and crashes.

1895 Otto Lilienthal adds controls to his gliders. He makes more than 2,000 flights in gliders of various shapes and sizes. He also tries wings that flap.

1896 Orville Wright almost dies of typhoid. The brothers learn of the death of Otto Lilienthal in a glider crash. They begin their study of flight.

1896 Samuel Pierpont Langley, head of the Smithsonian Institution in Washington, D.C., launches steam-powered model aeroplanes. His Aerodrome #5 flies well.

1897 In France, Clement Adler attempts to fly a machine with wings shaped like a bat's. It never leaves the ground and crashes on the second try.

1898 Alberto Santos-Dumont from Brazil builds the first lighter-than-air airship whose flight direction can be controlled.

1899 Wilbur Wright writes to the Smithsonian Institution requesting information about flight. He discovers the principle of wing warping. The brothers build and test a biplane kite.

1900 First flights of the Wrights' two-winged glider on the Outer Banks near Kitty Hawk are made in September and October.

1900 The first huge airships are built and flown by Count Ferdinand von Zeppelin in Germany.

1901 The Wrights return to Kitty Hawk and Kill Devil Hills in July and August. That fall, they use a wind tunnel and discover that the older tables of air pressure are wrong.

1901 Santos-Dumont flies a one-person airship around the Eiffel Tower in Paris.

1902 The Wright brothers test their glider near Kill Devil Hills in September and October. They begin building a lightweight aluminum motor in December.

1903 Samuel Langley's full-sized, manned Aerodrome is launched twice from a houseboat in the Potomac River, and twice it slides directly into the water.

1903 On December 17, Orville Wright completes the world's first powered, sustained, and controlled manned flight.

For Further Reading

Berliner, Don. *Aviation: Reaching for the Sky*. Minneapolis: The Oliver Press, 1997.

Freedman, Russell. *The Wright Brothers: How They Invented the Airplane*. New York: Holiday House, 1991.

Kelly, Fred C., ed. *Miracle at Kitty Hawk: The Letters of Wilbur and Orville Wright*. New York: Da Capo Press, 1996.

Old, Wendie. *The Wright Brothers: Inventors of the Airplane*. New Jersey: Enslow Publishers, 2000.

Wright, Orville. *How We Invented the Airplane, an Illustrated History*. New York: Dover Publications, 1988.

Notes

page 12
"I love to scrap with Orv . . ." is from Ivonette Wright Miller, "Character Study," in Ivonette Wright Miller, ed., *Wright Reminiscences* (Dayton, Ohio: The Air Force Museum Foundation, Inc., 1978), p. 61.

page 36
"After a while they shook hands . . ." is from Stephen Kirk, *First in Flight: The Wright Brothers in North Carolina* (Winston-Salem, N.C., John F. Blair Publisher, 1995), p. 179.

page 38
"I found myself caught in them wires . . ." is from Stephen Kirk, *First in Flight: The Wright Brothers in North Carolina*. (Winston-Salem, N.C., John F. Blair Publisher, 1995), p. 182.

page 41
"Success four flights Thursday . . ." is from Ivonette Wright Miller, "Speech Given by Ivonette Miller at the Luncheon to Commemorate the 100th Birthday Anniversary of Orville Wright," in Ivonette Wright Miller, ed., *Wright Reminiscences* (Dayton, Ohio: The Air Force Museum Foundation, Inc., 1978), p. 73.

Index